Opening up Community

The United Kingdom is a diverse country and, as the Census now ... is a large part of the population who profess to belong to differen... communities. There are also large numbers of people who choose to live their lives without religious beliefs. RE is for pupils who do not identify with a faith tradition as much as for those with a faith background. In RE therefore we need to consider appropriate alternative belief systems to religion which exist in the UK today.

This curriculum book explores three religion and belief systems that are represented in the primary schools of our country: Buddhism, Humanism and Sikhism. The articles focus on what it is to be part of a community of shared beliefs and ideas and how that affects the way people within these communities choose to live their lives.

The unit for 4–6 year olds uses some simple teaching from Buddhism, embracing images, story and active learning. For older children, two interviews support an enquiry about what it means to be part of a Buddhist community. The unit on Humanism for 7–11s looks at marriage and ethics. Younger children enquire into the Sikh community, looking at the key belief in sewa (service), and then older children are set a Mystery around how the Sikh community celebrate Baisakhi.

For the subject leader we have provided a set of pages to improve teachers' understanding of these three religion and belief communities and to support teaching about and from these communities accurately and appropriately. We are grateful to our religion and belief community consultants: Joyce Miller (Buddhism), Mike Lake (Humanism) and Mandeep Rattan (Sikh).

Fiona Moss

Web links: RE Today website

The RE Today website offers subscribers some free additional resources and classroom-ready materials related to this publication. Look out for the 'RE Today on the web' logo at the end of selected articles.

To access resources:

- go to the RE Today website www.retoday.org.uk

- click on the **download login** button and use the password from this term's issue of *REtoday* magazine

- click on **Primary curriculum publication – web supplement**

- click on the title of the publication and scroll down the page to find what you are looking for.

Contents

RE Today
Services

1

What can Buddhists learn from the world around them? What can we learn?

For the teacher

This unit focuses on some simple messages from the Buddha's teachings, known as the Dhamma or Dharma. Many Buddhist texts use vivid imagery, similes and metaphors to help people learn from the natural world. This unit takes some of these ideas and helps young children to think about, talk about and explore these ideas with their bodies.

The simple messages from Buddhism include:

- be kind
- have a calm mind
- let go of greedy thoughts
- get rid of angry thoughts and feelings
- speak kind words to others.

Using the pages

There are several ways to use the resources in this unit:

- **explore one page at a time**, following the instructions at the top of each page
- **explore one image at a time**, taking the image from page 3 and the corresponding instructions from pages 4–7
- do **a combination** of the two, selecting some images rather than using all eight.

You will need to photocopy, laminate and cut up several sets of the cards from pages 3–4, one for each group of children. All the instructions needed can be found on each page.

The following resources are available for subscribers to download from the RE Today website:

- Learning from nature: image cards (page 3)
- Learning from nature: matching (page 4)
- Learning from nature: use your body! (page 5)
- Learning from nature: lessons from Buddhism (page 6)
- Learning from nature: taking it further (page 7).

See: www.retoday.org.uk/supplements

What can children do as a result of this unit?

This article supports children working within the Early Learning goals outlined below, and the pupil friendly 'I can ' statements for level 1 and 2 describe what older or more able pupils may achieve through this work.

Early Learning goals	These activities help young children to
	• develop respect for different beliefs
	• use language to imagine and create roles and experiences
	• use talk to organise, sequence and clarify thinking, ideas, feelings and events
	• respond in a variety of ways to what they see, hear, smell, touch and feel.
Level 1	**I can . . .** • **recognise** three things Buddhists learn from looking at the world around them • *talk about* what I think is good about being kind and calm.
Level 2	**I can . . .** • *create* two examples from nature that would show what Buddhists believe about being kind and calm • *talk about* how we can use our bodies to learn about how to live.

A final creative activity

After engaging the children with the images, teaching and activities, use this creative activity to capture some of the children's learning.

Ask children to

- suggest some other things from nature and lessons we might learn from them. Some could link to the Buddhist teachings; some could be children's own ideas for how we should behave.
- **choose** two of these creatures or objects from nature for themselves.
  - one can be the kind of person they already are.
  - one can be the kind of person they would like to be.
- **create** a drawing or painting of the two creatures/objects they have chosen. Alternatively, **for writers**, a simple writing frame could help:

I am like a . . . because . . .

I want to be more like a . . . because . . .

A (e.g. stream) is (lively). I am/am not like this.

RE Today Services

Learning from nature: image cards

All of these images draw on Buddhist scriptures.

Give groups of children a set of images each and talk with them about what they can see. Ask them to come up with a simple caption for each picture, then share the captions listed opposite.

1. Cool glass of water
2. Deep calm lake
3. Greedy fat pig
4. Silly monkey stuck on tar
5. Fragrant flower
6. Bowl of water
7. Hen sitting on her eggs
8. Bee taking nectar

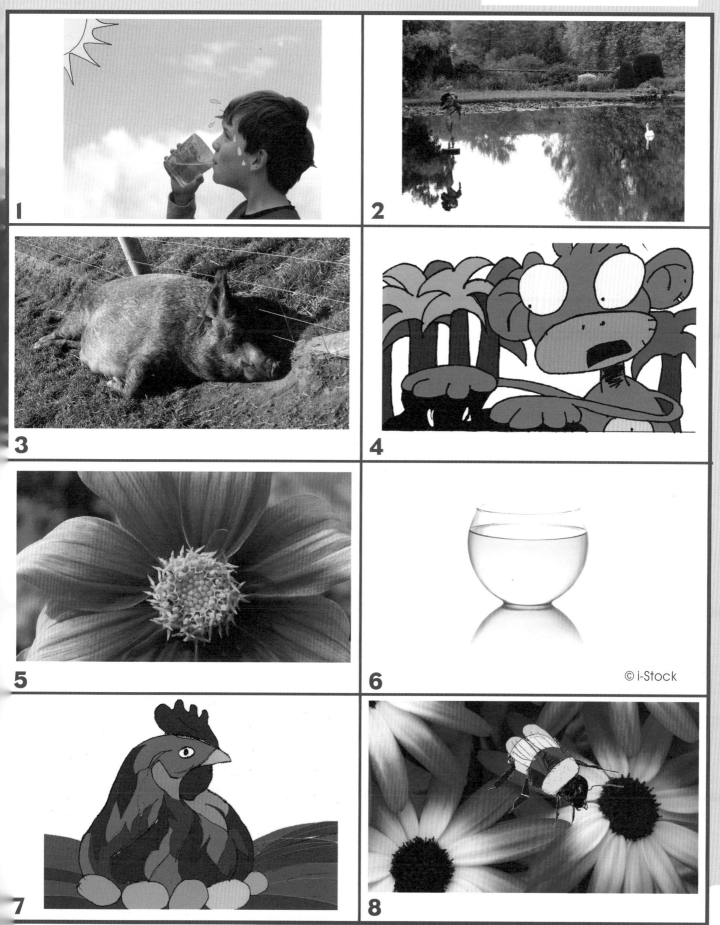

© i-Stock

RE Today Services

Learning from nature: matching

Read one card at a time to the children and ask them which image the words connect with.

- **Ask** children to hold up the image from their set.
- **Ask** them why it matches.

There may be different links, so accept different answers, but the ones this unit is drawing out match the placing of the images in the grid on page 3.

When they have made a connection with an image, you might like to try the 'use your body' activity from page 5.

Refreshing!	**Peaceful and still**
Lazy and sleepy	**Foolish – caught in a sticky trap**
Smells so lovely!	**Still and clear**
Being patient	**Taking nectar but doing no harm**

RE Today Services

Learning from nature: use your body!

The Buddhist teachings ask followers to learn something from nature. These activities help to make the learning exciting and fun, making a link with children's own experiences. If they **act out** some of these ideas, they will be better able to understand the Buddhist teachings from page 6.

Act out this picture. Pretend it's a really, really hot day. How does it feel? How do you act?

You're hot and really thirsty. Someone gives you a cool glass of water. The ice chinks against the glass. Drink it down. Feel it cold on your teeth . . . down your throat . . . into your stomach. Ahh!

Why does this feel good?

Show a picture of a beautiful lake scene. Ask children to close their eyes and imagine that they are by the lake in the image. Imagine walking around the edge of the lake. Imagine being on a boat on the water. How does it feel to have the sun on your back?

Ask the children to open their eyes when they are ready and talk about the experience.

Imagine all you do all day is sit around, eating, eating, eating. Act out sitting on a sofa, filling yourself with food all day long. How do you feel? How do your clothes feel? Think about what it would be like to do this again tomorrow . . . and the next day.

Ask children to act out this story:

Now, a monkey sees some sticky tar and puts one paw into it. He thinks, 'That's ok, I can pull it out using my other paw.' So he puts his second paw in and it gets stuck too.

He thinks, 'That's ok, I can pull it out with my foot.' So he puts his foot in . . . and that gets stuck as well.

He thinks, 'I'll pull myself out using my other foot.' But that gets stuck. 'I'll use my mouth . . .' Guess what happens? Stuck there, whimpering, he cannot escape when the hunter arrives . . .

Bring in some fragrant flowers.

Ask the children: Can you smell them? Can you smell them all over the classroom?

See how the smell spreads across the room.

Imagine a kind word is like the smell of flowers. How can a kind word spread? How does that make you feel? What does that make you think about?

Bring in a large glass bowl. Put some coloured glass beads or shells in the bottom. Put in some mud or soil from the garden. Swirl the water round so that it is all muddy and cloudy.

Sit with the children and let the mud and water settle. Can they see the glass beads/shells now?

Ask the children: What does this make you think about? Are you like this sometimes? How? Is your mind all stirred up like this sometimes?

Show a picture of a broody hen incubating her eggs, or watch a video of one as her chicks hatch.

See http://bit.ly/Jv4lzg

See http://bit.ly/I6Pf8x

Talk about the hen's role, sitting patiently, warming the eggs until the chicks are ready to emerge.

What comments and questions do the children have?

What can we learn from the hen?

Go outside. Look at the flowers in the school garden. (Or alternatively watch a video - there are several clips on www.youtube.com.) Can you see some bees or other insects? Can you tell where a bee has been? How do you know?

If someone walked through the flowers, what would you see? How might someone behave badly to the flowers? What is different between the way the bee acts and ways people act?

What's the difference between being harmful and being harmless?

Learning from nature: lessons from Buddhism

These sayings are simple versions of what Buddhist scriptures say.

You might read one out and ask children to say which image from nature, and which 'use your body' activity, connects with it.

The boxes on page 7 give some extra information and ideas to help you discuss these teachings.

You should refresh other people by bringing love and kindness to everyone.

from Milindapanha 22.7

Listening to the words of the Buddha can bring you deep peace.

from Dhammapada 82

You cannot learn wise living if you are lazy and sleepy all the time.

from Dhammapada 325

Your mind is easily trapped by being greedy and angry. You should not get caught in these traps! Think clearly about what is happening to you!

from Samyutta Nikaya 47.7

A kind word is beautiful to others. It does good to other people.

from Dhammapada 51

Take time to be still and calm your thoughts.

It will help you to think more clearly.

from Dhammapada 34

Be patient. Do the right thing. Good can come.

from Majjhima Nikaya 53

Do not harm any living beings.

from Dhammapada 49

RE Today
Services

Learning from nature: taking it further

The information on this grid expands and explains the summaries of Buddhist scripture on page 6.

Choose some of these suggestions for exploring the ideas further with children.

After exploring the ideas further, there is a suggestion for a final activity on page 2.

The teaching of the Buddha says that Buddhists should practise becoming more kind and loving. They should give kindness and love to others. This will help them to refresh other people in a busy world.

Ask the children to come up with two ways they can be kind to each other, to their family, and to people around them.

How can they be kind to people they do not like very much?

The deep water of the lake stays still even when the storms blow. They only affect the surface of the water. Most Buddhists believe that, with practice in meditation, they can stay calm and peaceful even in difficult times.

Talk about times when it is difficult to be calm. How could thinking about the image of the lake help in these moments?

Buddhism teaches that there are some ways of living that do no one any good. Being lazy is one of these. You will not become wise if you don't put the effort in.

Ask the children what they might miss out on in life if they are always lazy.

Most Buddhists believe that we are easily distracted by things that look good – we want them! We are also upset when we don't get what we want. We can be greedy! Like the silly monkey, if we live like this, we waste our lives. We should let go of greedy and angry thoughts.

Talk about some things that people sometimes want but that don't make them happy. Do we behave like the silly monkey?!

The Buddha taught that one way to live well is to make sure that we do not use any words that hurt other people. We should find kind words to say instead. If we practise this a lot, we will find it easier and easier to say kind things. This will bring joy to others.

Talk with the children about what kind words they could use. Why is this a good thing to do?

Many Buddhists would say that we are very busy and our thoughts are often a bit of a whirlwind! Sitting calmly, thinking about breathing in and out – this can help us to make our thoughts quiet. This can help us to see things more clearly.

Ask the children if their thoughts are ever like whirlwind. Is it easy to calm them down?

A Buddhist story says that the hen doesn't realise that sitting on the eggs will make them hatch. She is just doing the right thing. So some Buddhists say that even if we don't understand mysteries of life, if we do the right thing, this can lead to good things. We must be good and be patient.

Talk to the children about what they think 'doing the right thing' would involve.

A key teaching of Buddhism is to do no harm to any living being. The bee does its job and serves the flower without harming it at all.

Ask the children what kinds of things we might do that harm other people and the world. How might we live differently – in ways that would not harm others and the world?

WHY IS HELPING PEOPLE IMPORTANT TO SIKHS?

For the teacher

The concept of **seva or selfless service** is at the heart of Sikhism. The activities in this section provide practical ways of engaging children with this concept, introducing them to Sikhism, and encouraging them to reflect on the value of helping others.

Activity 1 draws on a series of picture cards which can be used in a variety of ways to stimulate discussion and questions through presenting examples of helpfulness or service.

The images are available for subscribers to download from RE Today website.

Activity 2 encourages the class use of ICT (blogging and tweeting) to investigate the ways in which a wide variety of people help others, and their reasons. This provides a base from which children can consider what they are learning about seva, and also reflect on their own experience of and attitude to helping others.

Activity 3 uses a well-known story from the life of one of the Sikh Gurus to show the importance of sharing a meal together and of treating everyone equally. The text of the story is provided and a drama-based activity is suggested.

Activity 4 introduces pupils to the langar – a community meal provided by all Sikh communities and open to everyone, of any religion or none. Visual stimulus is suggested and a visit to a gurdwara is encouraged so that children can experience the hospitality of the Sikh community for themselves. An activity sheet provides a focus for thinking, and children are encouraged to look for links between the langar, and their learning in Activities 1, 2 and 3.

Curriculum links

Spiritual development: showing an interest in and respect for different people's feelings and values.

PSHCE: working with others, discussing beliefs, values and practices, collaborating with others and developing respect and sensitivity.

Literacy: speaking; listening and responding; use of faith story; group discussion and interaction.

What can children do as a result of this unit?

The following pupil friendly 'I can' statements describe the learning that may be expected of pupils in the 5–7 age range.

Level   Description of achievement: I can. . .

1
- **talk about** something Sikhs do to help other people
- **respond to questions** arising from a story about helping other people
- *talk about* why helping people is a good idea.

2
- **compose appropriate** questions to ask a Sikh
- **retell** a story told about one of the Gurus in words and drama and say how it recalls the Guru's teachings
- *respond* with thoughts of my own to the story and situations and **suggest why** being helpful to other people is important.

See also

1   **Picture gallery of seva (selfless service)**
    See: http://bit.ly/wtfxJf

2   **BBC Learning Zone Broadband Clips Library**

    A vast searchable database of short video clips including many topics studied in RE, including:
    - Sikh Food – clip 490
    - Sikh beliefs and worship – clip 3777

    See: www.bbc.co.uk/learningzone/clips

3   **Picture gallery about the langar**
    See: http://bit.ly/yAI1kE

4   **SikhNet Stories for Children**

    A growing collection of Sikh stories told for children by Sikh storytellers.
    See: www.sikhnet.com/stories

Activity 1
Introducing seva (selfless service)

Copy and cut out the cards on pages 10 and/or 11 (also available for subscribers of the RE Today website), making a set for each group of children, depending on the age of the children.

1 **Ask children to look at the cards** and decide in each case

   a the benefits of the help being offered

   b the consequences of no help being offered.

2 **Explain** that for Sikhs it is very important to help – or serve – other people whenever they can, even if it means putting themselves out. This is called **seva or selfless service**.

3 **Ask** the children to sort them into two piles things that they might say or do and things that they don't or wouldn't say or do.

4 **Ask children to suggest** why they think Sikhs try to help or serve people in the ways shown in the pictures.

5 **Show** children the photographs illustrating **seva** in this picture gallery http://bit.ly/wtfxJf

• What questions do they have about seva?

• What connections can they see between these photographs and the cards they sorted, e.g. the boy helping his father clean shoes / the Sikh man cleaning the shoes of worshippers in the gurdwara.

• What sort of seva do Sikhs do?

Activity 3   A story about Guru Amar Das and Emperor Akbar

1 **Tell the story** of Emperor Akbar's meeting with Guru Amar Das, page 12. Explain to children that a guru is a teacher, and that Sikhs have 10 human gurus, plus the Guru Granth Sahib which is a source of teaching now that the Gurus are no longer on earth.

2 **Talk** with children about the main characters in the story – their actions and feelings. Use a **feelings box** or a make a **feelings graph** to support the discussion. Feelings might include: kind, strong, holy, happy, caring, in charge, thoughtful, puzzled, hopeful, sad, proud.

3 **Act out** the story in groups of three or four.

4 **Decide** together which scene is the most important one in the story and freeze-frame the story at that point.

5 **Talk** with children about these questions:

• Why did Emperor Akbar agree to eat with everyone?

• What did they talk about after the meal?

Activity 2   Blogs and tweets

Class blogs and Twitter are excellent ways of bringing into the RE classroom a variety of perspectives to stimulate discussion and deepen understanding.

• Talk to the colleagues in your school who blog and tweet (it may be you!). Ask them to post a simple question about serving or helping other people, ideally devised by your class, e.g. 'What sort of things have you done to help someone else this week – and why?'

• Raise awareness of the blog via a class Twitter account.

• Let pupils log on from time to time during the day to see the responses as they are received. Looking for the most frequently offered reasons for helping someone else will be a fruitful stimulus to class discussion.

Activity 4   The langar

1 **Introduce** children to the langar – the community kitchen which is an expression of the concept of 'selfless service' integral to the life of all Sikh communities. Using the activity sheet on page 13, ask them to look at the picture closely and suggest their questions and responses to the sentence starts provided.

2 **Show** children 'Sikh Food' (Clip 490 from the BBC's Learning Zone Clips Library) and/or the picture gallery on http://bit.ly/yAl1kE. Have their questions been answered? What new questions do they have? What links can they make between what they learned in Activities 1, 2 and 3 – and what they now know about the langar? Prompt questions might include:

• In what sorts of ways do Sikhs try to serve other people?

• Why is serving other people important to Sikhs?

• Why do Sikhs today still have the langar?

• What does the langar tell us about how Sikhs regard other people?

3 **Choose** one photograph or scene from the video clip – and ask children what they imagine is going on behind the photographer or film maker, or on the other side of a door or through a window.

4 **Visit** a local gurdwara, so that children can see for themselves where the langar takes place, and talk with members of the Sikh community about why happens and why it is so important to them.

RE Today
Services

Pictures: Set 2

9

The Guru Granth Sahib says: 'No one is my enemy and no one is a stranger. I get along with everyone.'

10

Sikhs in Norwich get ready to open their new gurdwara.

11

Sikhs in America give away free winter coats to the needy.

12

The best way to live, I think, is to share, get on with people, and look after people.

13

The best way to live is to pray every day and to help everyone who comes your way, so that these will be counted in your favour by God.

14

Sikhs in London collect food for the homeless.

Emperor Akbar meets Guru Amar Das

Guru Nanak, the first Sikh Guru

Guru Angad, the second Sikh Guru

Guru Amar Das, the third Sikh Guru

At the time of Guru Amar Das, the third Sikh Guru, the ruler of India was the Emperor Akbar. He was a wise and good emperor. He thought very highly of holy men, respected the different religions that there were in India, and was interested in what the different holy books had to say.

One day Emperor Akbar decided to go and visit Guru Amar Das, the third Sikh Guru. Normally when the Emperor went to visit people, they went to a lot of trouble to make sure that everything was done properly, and that he was treated as a very important visitor. However Guru Amar Das refused to see him until he had eaten food in the langar.

The Guru, the Emperor and all the other people who were there sat down together in lines on the floor. It made no difference how much money a person had, or how powerful they were, or how clever they were. They all sat down together and ate the same food, even the great Emperor Akbar.

In this way everyone was reminded that they were equal and that God gives good things to everyone.

Guru Amar Das was impressed by the way Emperor Akbar behaved. He could see that he was a good and honest man. After the meal, the two men met and spoke together.

Why do you think Emperor Akbar agreed to eat with everyone?

What do you think they talked about after the meal?

RE Today
Services

Thinking about the langar

Another question we have is . . .

We are not sure about . . .

It's made us think about . . . .

Our deepest thoughts about the picture are . . .

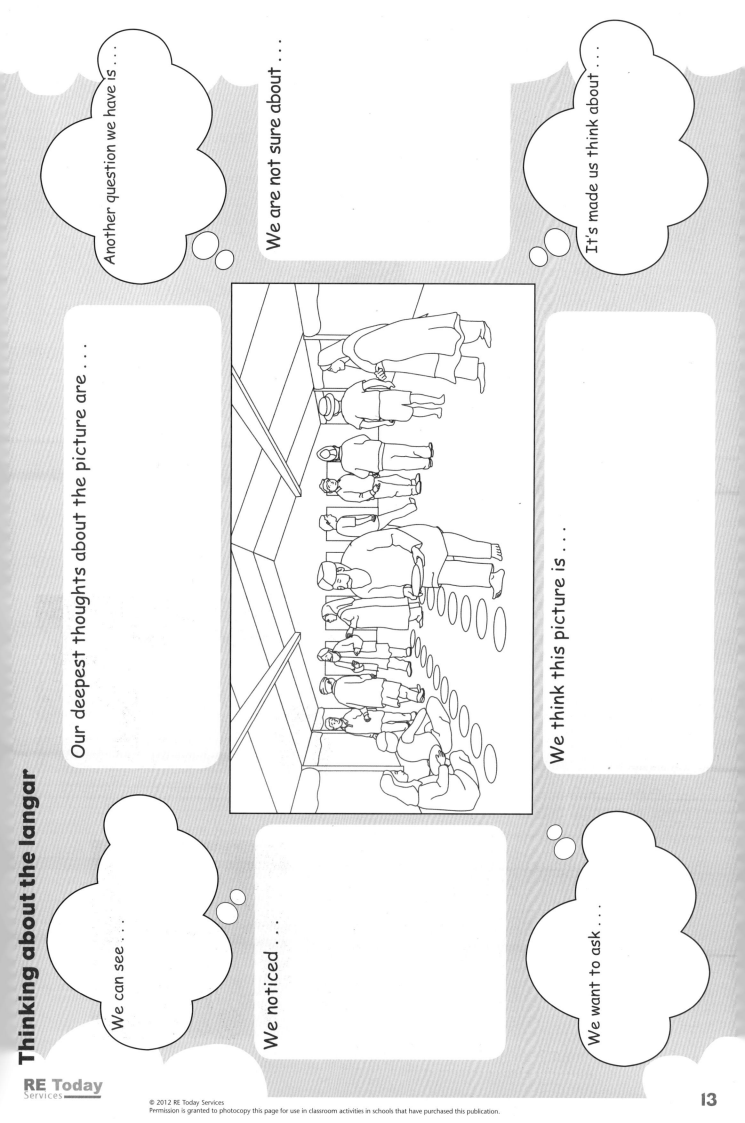

We think this picture is . . .

We can see . . . .

We noticed . . . .

We want to ask . . . .

How and why do Sikhs celebrate Baisakhi?

For the teacher

The story of the formation of the Khalsa in 1699 and the contemporary celebration of Baisakhi (Vaisakhi) are events close to the heart of all Sikhs, no matter how 'religious' or 'secular' they consider themselves to be.

The resources and activities in this section enable pupils aged 7–9 years to understand the importance and impact of the festival story (page 16) on believers today, and the ways in which Baisakhi is celebrated as an inclusive community event.

There is also opportunity for pupils to reflect on questions of commitment and making and keeping promises – how are the everyday lives of individuals affected when a serious commitment is made? What promises and commitments have pupils made for themselves and what thoughts do they have about these?

What can children do as a result of this unit?

The following pupil friendly 'I can' statements describe the learning that may be expected of pupils in the 7–9 age range.

Level Description of achievement: I can. . .

2
- **retell** the story of Baisakhi
- *respond* sensitively to some questions about the story of Baisakhi.

3
- **link up** the story of Baisakhi to ways Sikhs celebrate today; **suggest meanings** for what happens in the story
- *make links* between what I celebrate and what Sikhs celebrate; talk about attitudes to giving things up.

4
- **show** that I understand what Baisakhi, Amrit and the Five Ks have to do with commitment
- *use* my understanding of Sikh commitment to reflect on my own commitments.

See also

1 **BBC Learning Zone Broadband Clips Library**

A vast searchable database of short video clips including many topics studied in RE, including:

- Origin of the Khalsa – clip 672
- Baisakhi in the Gurdwara – clip 673
- Baisakhi the Sikh new year – clip 4803
- The meaning of the Five Ks – clip 4805
- Explanation of Khanda and Khalsa – clip 4806
- The Guru Granth Sahib – clip 4825

See: www.bbc.co.uk/learningzone/clips

2 **Sikhnet Stories for Children**

A growing collection of Sikh stories told for children by Sikh storytellers.

See: www.sikhnet.com/stories

3 **CLEO**

A large collection of short videos filmed specifically for the RE classroom including several focusing on the Guru Granth Sahib.

See: www.cleo.net.uk/resources

4 **Sikhs.org**

A straightforward website covering Sikh origins, teaching, beliefs and way of life.

See: http://sikhs.org

The road is swept clean in readiness for the Guru Granth Sahib's arrival

The Guru Granth Sahib arrives

RE Today
Services

Activity 1
The formation of the Khalsa

1 As a whole class activity **create a mind map** around the word 'Commitment'. To prompt ideas **ask** pupils to suggest:

- alternative words for commitment, e.g. devotion

- what people can be committed to, e.g. a football team, their family, a hobby, their religion, music

- how people show their commitment, e.g. words, actions, how they spend their money, the job they do. Does commitment always lead to action?

- what people might give up or even die for – and why. Can they think of any stories or real-life examples?

- what are pupils committed to and how do they show it?

2 **Read Davinder's story**, page 16, with the class – about how the Khalsa started. Working in small groups, ask the class to identify a key moment in the story and to **freeze-frame** that scene. They should think about what each character is thinking and feeling and share their ideas.

A digital camera can be used to capture the freeze-frames. Pupils can express the thoughts and feelings of the characters in speech and thought bubbles added to the digital image.

3 **Revisit the mind map** – and amend it / add to it in light of the freeze-frame activity. **Ask** pupils:

- Is commitment to God different from other kinds of commitment? How? Why?

- What other stories about commitment to God do they know? Why are these stories remembered?

Activity 2
Celebrating Baisakhi – a Mystery

1 A Mystery is a thinking skills strategy that provides a structure through which pupils can:

- **sort** relevant from irrelevant information

- **interpret** information

- **make** links between different pieces of information

- **speculate** to form hypotheses

- **check, refine** and **explain**

- **talk about** their learning and thinking processes.

2 Prepare a set of the cards on pages 17 and 18 for each group of up to four pupils. Include the central question that pupils have to answer: **Why were 5000 people walking through the streets of Leicester in April?**

Explain to pupils that they need to:

- **find** an answer to the central question (there is not necessarily a right answer)

- **sort** through the clues in their set of cards, and **decide** whether they contribute to an answer to the question. Some of the clues are red herrings.

- move the cards around the table as they **discuss, decide, explain, prioritise and refine** their thinking

- **share** with the whole class their answer to the question and **justify** their reasons.

3 Provide an opportunity for pupils to debrief the activity itself, focusing on how it helped them in their thinking.

Activity 3   Important promises
To think and talk about

1 Look at the five promises made by Sikhs when they join the Khalsa, page 18. What sort of lifestyle do you think a devoted Sikh would live today?

2 If you had to make five important promises, what would they be? How do you think these promises would affect your everyday life?

Baisakhi – the formation of the Khalsa

Davinder's Story

A fictionalised first-person account of the Baisakhi story.

Let me introduce myself. I'm a 14-year-old girl and my name is Davinder Kaur – well, it is now! Let me tell you how it changed.

Last month it was a special festival for us Sikhs. Our guru, who's called **Guru Gobind Rai**, sent a message round to us all to make a big effort to go to Anandpur for the festival. Our family had to walk for two days to get there. But I'm glad we went.

You should have seen it: there were huge crowds, and people all up the hill, with a tent at the top. Our Guru is a wonderful speaker. He gave a speech that day that was to change all our lives.

We stood quite far back, but I had a good view. He was reminding us about being committed to the Sikh path, and ended up asking who would give something up for the faith. People offered money, time, and all sorts of different gifts – animals, and even a house (Sikhs are supposed to be generous).

Then the Guru lifted his head and spoke again: 'But who among you will give your life, your head, to show your commitment?' He brandished a sword. His eyes gleamed.

The crowds fell silent, shocked, for what seemed like ages. The breeze fluttered the tent. Then, quietly, a man stepped forward. 'I'm prepared to die for my faith,' he said, softly. The Guru led him into the tent. The crowd stayed silent. There was a sickening sound from inside, a sort of thud.

Then the Guru came out again, with blood on his sword and his clothes. He called for another person willing to die for the faith. I tugged at Dad's jacket and whispered, 'He didn't kill him, did he, Dad?' My dad motioned me to be silent. I couldn't believe what I was seeing.

But a second person did step forward. Into the tent he went. We heard the thudding chop of a sword, blood splashed onto the tent from inside. The Guru did this five times altogether, with the crowd growing more and more uncomfortable. He seemed to be inside for ages.

Then the flap opened, and the Guru walked out. Behind him came the five men. Suddenly the horrified silence broke. Everyone was gasping and crying, going crazy.

At last, the Guru got us all to listen again, and praised the five. We were all wondering what had happened inside, and what he had said – had he just been beheading some animals, goats or something? Had the five men been killed, and been brought back to life by a miracle?

We didn't get answers, but we did get a challenge. Guru Gobind Rai told us that he wanted more commitment from all of us. He named the five men as **Panj Piare** (it means The Beloved Five), and asked us all to join him in becoming **Khalsa**.

He prepared a bowl of water, in which his wife Mata Sundri sprinkled sugar crystals. He sprinkled this **amrit** from the iron bowl onto the eyes and heads of the five brave people, and each one showed their commitment. Again we gasped as the Guru himself bowed down before these Five.

We shouldn't have been surprised, I suppose – he is a humble Guru. He then gave them five symbols to wear, and new names. He said Sikh men should add **Singh** (Lion) to their names, and Sikh women should add **Kaur** (Princess) to theirs.

I can't really explain how we were feeling on the way home. Dad seemed very quiet. My sister was quite tearful. But we've all decided we are all going to be much more committed than we have been before. It was a great day, and very emotional.

And now my guru is called **Guru Gobind Singh**, and my name is Davinder Kaur.

RE Today
Services

Why were 5000 people walking through the streets of Leicester in April?

Guru Nanak was the first Sikh Guru.	Guru Gobind Rai wanted all Sikhs to show more commitment to the Sikh way of life.	Sikhs are expected to be generous e.g. with their time, skills, money and hospitality.
The first Baisakhi festival took place in 1699 CE.	At the first Baisakhi, five men showed that they were willing to die to demonstrate their commitment to their religion.	Guru Gobind Rai knelt before the Panj Piare.
Panj Piare means The Beloved Five.	In the gurdwaras in Leicester there are readings from the Guru Granth Sahib.	Guru Gobind Rai's wife was called Mata Sundri.
Baisakhi is a chance for everyone to dress up in their best clothes.	The Guru Granth Sahib is the Sikh holy book.	In Leicester each year there is a big festival to celebrate Baisakhi.
The five men who offered their lives at the first Baisakhi were called the Panj Piare.	Baisakhi celebrates the setting up of the Sikh religion as we know it today.	About 12,000 Sikhs live in Leicester.
In 1699 Guru Gobind Rai urged all Sikhs to go to Anandpur for the harvest festival.	The Khalsa was set up at the first Baisakhi. The first members were the Panj Piare.	Any Sikh who has been through the Amrit ceremony is a member of the Khalsa.

RE Today Services

Guru Gobind Rai sprinkled sugared water called amrit on the eyes and heads of the Panj Piare.

Not all Sikhs are members of the Khalsa. All Sikhs are welcome at Baisakhi.

Guru Gobind Rai set Sikhs a challenge – to show their commitment to God.

Towns in the UK with significant numbers of Sikhs

Sikh men dressed as the Five Panj Piare

Those joining the Khalsa make five promises:

- **To wear the 5 Ks**
- **To follow the teaching of the Ten Gurus and the Guru Granth Sahib**
- **To accept responsibility for service to the Khalsa**
- **To abstain from alcohol, tobacco and to respect women**
- **To work hard and to give to charity**

God always looks after the weak, protects believers and destroys evil.

Guru Gobind Singh, the tenth Guru

The Guru Granth Sahib travels in a procession through Leicester

The Khanda - symbol of Sikhism

RE Today Services

WHAT IS IMPORTANT FOR BUDDHISTS ABOUT BEING PART OF A COMMUNITY?

For the teacher

This unit for 9–11s focuses on the concept of community within Buddhism. Like most religious believers, Buddhists are encouraged to meet together to learn and act out their beliefs.

The Sangha is the spiritual community of Buddhists. Some Buddhists use this term only to refer to the ordained Buddhist monks and nuns while others use it to refer to lay and ordained Buddhists.

At the heart of this unit of learning is a rich resource: two interviews with practising Buddhists. We have suggested a series of activities, but this original oral resource could be used in many other explorations or enquiries into Buddhism.

The activities for 9–11-year-olds give pupils the opportunity to explore their own understanding of community actively by playing a game, through discussion and reflecting on a story from Buddhist sacred text. The unit links closely with literacy teaching as the pupils actively read the interviews, enquire into community in Buddhism and create discussion or explanatory texts.

See also

1 **CLEO Buddhist video cards**

   Four Buddhists answer questions about their beliefs and ideas.

   See: www.cleo.net.uk/

2 **BBC Learning Zone Broadband Clips Library**

   A vast searchable database of short video clips including many topics studied in RE, including:

   • Martin becomes a monk – clip 3785
   • Buddhist prayer and meditation – clip 2872

   See: www.bbc.co.uk/learningzone/clips

3 **Sangha day**

   This Buddhist festival is an opportunity for Buddhists to reaffirm their commitment. It is not celebrated by all Buddhist communities.

   See: www.bbc.co.uk/religion/religions/

   See: www.mindfulmum.co.uk/fun/2011/sangha day-for-kids/

4 **Ask a Buddhist**

 • This website from Clear Vision Trust has a series of short videos in answer to commonly asked questions. It is for upper primary and secondary, so a wide variety of questions are answered. Some questions are not suitable for primary pupils.

   See: http://bit.ly/HQEx1c

What can children do as a result of this unit?

The following pupil-friendly 'I can' statements describe the learning that may be expected of pupils in the 9–11 age range.

Level	Description of achievement: I can. . .
3	• describe some similarities and differences between life as an ordained and lay Buddhist
	• *suggest answers a Buddhist might give about the importance of living as part of a community.*
4	• apply ideas from Buddhist teaching to examples of how different members of the Buddhist community support one another
	• *refer to ideas from the Buddhist Sangha to describe my idea of what a positive community is.*
5	• explain the impact of being part of the Buddhist Sangha on the way Buddhists live in their community and in the wider world
	• *explain my views on the positive and negative aspects of living as part of a religious community.*

The following resources are available for subscribers to download from the RE Today website

• The interviews with Munisha and Joyce on pages 20–21
• The pupil resource sheet for Activity 3 on page 23.

See: www.retoday.org.uk/supplements

Links across the curriculum

The work in this unit could be used as a context for literacy teaching on discussion or explanation texts.

Munisha

Munisha is an ordained Triratna Buddhist and works for a charity that helps people understand more about Buddhism.

What is your favourite piece of Buddhist teaching?

The Buddha taught that there is a thread of suffering running through everything in life, even through enjoyable things. He taught that nothing lasts for ever; everything changes. I know from experience that there is suffering in everything – brilliant films and ice creams come to an end. The teaching reminds me this is normal. It also means unpleasant experiences end too.

The Buddha also taught that actions have consequences. If everything I do makes a difference, I am not stuck with the way I am now. I can change and become kinder and happier, if I make the effort.

Why is community important to Buddhists?

The Buddha said that for the health of the Sangha it was important to meet regularly and in large numbers. My tradition, the Triratna Order, encourage everyone in the Sangha to form close friendships and spend time together, whether working, meditating, going on retreat or living together. This way we encourage each other to make progress in moving towards greater wisdom and compassion.

What do you actively have to do as part of your community?

I don't think Buddhists *have* to do anything; after all, Buddhism does not include worshipping a creator God, an external authority figure. In choosing to live a Buddhist life we are undertaking to do our best to live in certain ways, as a result of our own values.

In the Triratna tradition we expect people to do their best to live by five precepts in all situations. We expect most people to be vegetarian, meditate daily, go on retreat regularly, cultivate friendships and be helpful to others.

What does it mean to you to be a member of the Buddhist community?

It is tremendously important. It is hard for me to imagine what life is like for people who are not part of a worldwide community of people committed to the same values, doing the same meditations, encouraging each other to move towards wisdom and compassion, to change the world, person by person.

As an ordained Buddhist I'm part of a chapter of four ordained women who meet weekly at my house for a couple of hours to discuss our lives, to study and worship together. I also live with six ordained Buddhist women and share an office with four Buddhists!

What are the challenges of being in the Buddhist community?

It is a bit harder to get away with being irresponsible! Becoming a member of my Order, one of the things I committed to was being open with my fellow Order members, not being secretive. As an ordained Buddhist I do my best to live by 10 ethical precepts covering my behaviour, my communication, relationships and my mind.

I am open to being challenged about any of these and I'm committed to helping others by challenging them too – always in a kind and helpful way, of course!

RE Today
Services

Joyce

Joyce is a lay member of the Thai Forest Sangha within Theravada Buddhism. She used be a secondary school teacher in Coventry.

What is your favourite piece of Buddhist teaching?

The four Brahmaviharas or divine abidings are significant for me – they are developing loving kindness, compassion, sympathetic joy and equanimity (which is calmness and being even-tempered).

They are significant because that is the sort of person I would aspire to be if Buddhists had aspirations! I know that sounds a bit odd but grasping after goodness is still grasping – if you put too much energy into that then you're going to end up disappointed with yourself.

Why is community important to Buddhists?

Perhaps because it is important to all human beings – which I do think is true. That is why I like Buddhism – it seems to me to be true and the focus on community is a recognition that we are social beings and we need the spiritual and moral support that a community brings.

When we see people who are not part of a community it is obvious that most are suffering.

What does it mean to you to be a member of the Buddhist community?

Spiritual friendship is the main community focus for me. In Noble Silence particularly, that friendship with others can deepen in very significant ways. Noble Silence is what we observe formally when we are on a retreat and may not speak for up to 10 days.

Life slows down and awareness increases and that promotes the practice of mindfulness which is at the heart of leading a Buddhist life. By mindfulness, I mean deep awareness, which we try to develop through meditation.

What do you actively have to do as part of your community?

I'm not sure there is anything I *have* to do. Buddhism doesn't really have rules and demands. I attend a weekly meditation session, a monthly daily retreat and go on longer retreats, when I can observe the Precepts to the best of my ability.

They are the basis of Buddhist morality and make sense to me as the way in which I can avoid creating suffering for myself and others.

What are the challenges of being in the Buddhist community?

It is a challenge to practise patience and to maintain silence, rather than reacting immediately to something, especially when faced with aggression, for example.

It is also hard not to feel irritated when my mind is wandering during meditation. Meditation is a very difficult practice and it's important not to be judgemental about its outcomes.

Activity 1　A co-operation game

This game is designed a starter activity for this series of lessons as, in order to succeed, the children need to work together as a community.

The example below is a simple game that can be played in the classroom, but with time and imagination there are many co-operation games that can be played with string or planks of wood!

- Arrange the children into groups of four. Each group needs a hoop and a plastic cup. **Ask** all the children to stand in the hoop and place the cup 75 cm from the edge of the hoop.
- **Challenge** each group to pick up the cup without anyone stepping out of the hoop. After children have succeeded, move the cup slightly further away. Can they pick up the cup now?
- Give the pupils opportunity to talk in groups and then as a whole class to **discuss** what they have learnt from playing that game.
- Introduce the key question for the series of lessons:

  What is important for Buddhists about being part of a community?

Activity 3　Active reading to summarise and enquire

Introduce the pupils to the two Buddhist interviewees. Share with the children that both women have been Buddhists for many years. Munisha is an ordained member of the Sangha or community, which means she has taken a very deep level of commitment. Joyce is a member of a different Buddhist community and is not ordained but supports those who are by contributing to the running of a Buddhist monastery.

- **Ask** the children to work in pairs with one interview.
- **Explain** that their task is to give a one-minute summary of the key points of the interview to another pair who won't have read it.
- Share with the children the recording sheet on page 23. Some pairs will work better without a recording sheet and you may add extra sentences to the recording sheet to support some pupils.
- Allow pupils approximately ten minutes to **read** the interview and record their ideas.
- Match each pair with two pupils who have read the other interview and **share** the summaries.
- As a class, **share** what they have learnt about the unit question:

  What is important for Buddhists about being part of a community?

Activity 2
Communities - giving and getting

- **Ask** the children to list the communities that people in their area might belong to: for example, school, sports team, youth club, cub scout group, religious group.
- **Ask** pupils to work in talk partners:
  - Choose a community to think about
  - Suggest three things that you gain from being part of the community
  - Suggest three things you have to give to be a member of the community.
- **Ask** pupils to consider:

  Can you be part of a community and only give or only get?
- Share the story of Anuruddha and his friends. **Ask** the pupils to suggest what the Buddha might have valued about the way they lived in a community?

Anuruddha and his friends

Two and a half thousand years ago in India, there were three monks named Anuruddha, Kimbila and Nandiya. One day their teacher, the Buddha, turned up unexpectedly to see how they were getting on. They told him that they were quite happy: they appreciated each other's good qualities, and had a kindly regard for each other. 'How is it that you get on so well?' he asked them.

'Well,' said Anuruddha, 'I often think how lucky I am to be living a Buddhist life with such friends. I try to act kindly towards them. I try to speak kindly to them. I also try to think kindly about them. Sometimes when we disagree and want to do different things, I think, "Why not do what he wants, instead of what I want?"'

They explained how they ran their home: 'We go from house to house for our food each day. Whichever of us gets home first puts out seats, and water for drinking and washing; whoever comes home last clears away the meal, empties the bin and sweeps the floor. If any of us notices something needs doing around the place, he just does it. If he can't do it on his own, he asks us for help.'

These three friends never just thought, 'Oh, someone else will do it.'

From the Majjhima Nikaya. Reproduced from the *Buddhist Centre in The City* teacher's handbook, with the kind permission of the Clear Vision Trust.

RE Today Services

Enquiring into Buddhist community Name of interviewee:	An example of Buddhist teaching is . . . It is important because . . .	Community is important to Buddhists because . . .
As part of the Buddhist community, Munisha/Joyce	A challenge of being part of the community is . . .	Questions we want to ask or enquire into . . .

Activity 4   Enquiring into the importance of community for Buddhists

Enquiring

Discuss with the pupils the questions that they wanted to enquire into. If they struggle to generate questions for enquiry you could suggest questions or ask them to enquire into the celebration of Sangha day. There are many ways for pupils to gain answers to their enquiry questions: use of the internet, research or inviting a visitor into the classroom. The following resources might provide some responses.

Ask a Buddhist: This website from Clear Vision Trust has a series of short videos in answer to commonly asked questions. It is for upper primary and secondary and so a wide variety of questions are answered. The responses to the question 'What is the best thing about being a Buddhist?' from Amalavavajra, and Munisha and Jayadevi on 'What is the hardest thing about being a Buddhist?', are good places to start.
See: http://bit.ly/HQEx1c

Email a believer: This website has the facility for pupils to email a Buddhist and also lists answers to questions asked by other pupils.
See: http://pof.reonline.org.uk

Expressing and explaining

- **Ask** the pupils to choose either

  ° What is important for Buddhists about being part of a community? Or

  ° Is being part of a community important to Buddhists?

- **Ask** pupils to **write** either an explanation or discussion text to answer the question. Pupils can either produce a leaflet to go into the local library or write a short newspaper article for a young people's newspaper.

- The piece of work will need to include quotes from members of the Buddhist community, the pupils' opinions and ideas, and reference to some Buddhist teaching, for example the teaching chosen by the interviewees.

WHAT VIEWS AND IDEAS DO HUMANISTS HAVE?

For the teacher

RE is for all, in law, and so it should take the beliefs and values of all pupils – and the communities from which they come – seriously. Since 2004, government guidance on the scope of RE has made reference to 'religion and beliefs' as a way of recognising and including the non-religious beliefs of large proportions of our UK population. Many pupils, in almost every school, are non-religious by practice. They are not all Humanists with a capital 'H': many are spiritual and loosely identify with a religion.

The activities for 7–11s in this section of the book look at a Humanist wedding as a simple starting point for Humanist values work. Many Humanists are atheists, believing there is no such person as god. Some are agnostic about god – not sure if the question can be answered.

Information file

This section of the book explores how pupils can learn from Humanism. The work pictures many 7–11 year olds who have not heard the word 'Humanist' before, so the first piece of core knowledge is that there are many people who do not believe in god, but do believe in humanity. Some of these people call themselves 'Humanists'.

They are all different, many say 'I don't believe in religion, but **I do believe in morality, in doing good.**' 'I don't believe in life after death, but **I do believe in making the most of our days on earth.**' 'I don't believe in any gods or goddesses, but **I do believe in humanity.**' 'I don't believe in holy books or sacred writings, but **I do believe science can tell us about where we come from.**'

An excellent starting point for this work is to get children to write some 'I don't believe . . . but I do believe . . .' sentences of their own, and compare them with these Humanist examples.

See also

Local Humanist groups are often willing and able to provide a good school RE visitor. Find out if there is one near you, and invite them in.

The British Humanist Association offers two very useful sites for teachers and pupils. Choose the most primary-friendly sections for this

See: www.humanismforschools.org.uk
www.simpleguidetohumanism.org.uk

What can children do as a result of this unit?

The following pupil-friendly 'I can' statements describe the learning that may be expected of pupils in the 7–11 age range.

Level Description of achievement: I can. . .

2
- **use the right words to identify** some different things that matter to Humanists
- **ask lots of questions** about Humanists and **what matters** to them
- *respond sensitively to questions about living a non-religious way of life, e.g. do you think Humanists have found a good way to live?*

3
- **identify and describe** some values that matter to Humanists
- **describe** how a Humanist is different from a religious person
- list some **similarities and differences between** Humanists and religious people
- *make links between my own ideas about what matters most and Humanist values.*

4
- **use the right words to show that I understand** how and why Humanists reject beliefs about God, afterlife or holy books
- *respond thoughtfully to questions about the values that matter to Humanists, applying ideas for myself.*

The following resources are available for subscribers to download from the RE Today website

- A simple PowerPoint sequence to support the learning in this unit
- A recording sheet for page 29 Activity 6b: A values auction

See: www.retoday.org.uk/supplements

Links across the curriculum

The activities in this section of the book have good links to literacy work for 9–11s. Pupils commonly learn about persuasive writing in Year 5, in England, and about argument in Year 6. These studies and related speaking and listening skills connect RE to Literacy and can gain extra time for focusing pupils' learning in RE.

Activity 1   When Humanists get married

Begin by asking children about where weddings happen. They may list lots of different places, including religious buildings.

Teach the class that although religious people like to marry in gurdwaras and churches, and think of God as one of their wedding guests, lots of people are non-religious. A wedding can happen in a hotel, stately home or register office, as well as in a religious building.

Ask children to:

- suggest advantages and disadvantages to a wedding in a religious building and a wedding in a non-religious setting
- suggest who might prefer a non-religious wedding.

Show pupils the picture below, available for RE today subscribers on the PowerPoint that accompanies this article. **Ask** them to think about the questions below.

- What are they thinking?
- What will they promise?
- Why do people marry?

> Thanks to Mike Lake, a Humanist school visitor and member of Derby SACRE for his help with this article. He comments: 'Atheist Humanists don't believe in the supernatural, god or a soul, but do come together to celebrate the great moments in life. We believe that the purpose of life is to be happy and to help others to be happy.'

The answers to these questions are likely to be full of values words: love, kindness, enjoying company, planning to have children and caring for each other, for example. Collect these words from the children.

Tell children that the Humanist wedding is one example of how some people like to live their lives without religion and god. A Humanist is a person who believes in 'Good without God'. Tell them they are going to be finding out about what matters to Humanists in the next few lessons.

Humanist Mike Lake suggests not all 'non-religious' people identify themselves as Humanists. Remind pupils that non-religious communities are diverse, just like religious communities.

© Anne-Marie Palmer/Alamy

Explain to pupils that this is a photo from a Humanist wedding, where there will be no prayers, hymns or vicars. Instead, love poetry, the couple's favourite songs or music, and the community of their friends and family, will celebrate their marriage.

Ask pupils who would choose a wedding like this, and what would make it a special occasion. They might **identify some similarities and differences** between religious and non-religious weddings.

RE Today
Services

Activity 2
Do rules matter? Why? What is a code for living?

Screen Baddies: what's wrong with them?

Ask pupils to choose three 'villains' from stories, films or TV series that they love.

- What makes these people bad?
- What rules do they break?
- What does their breaking of a code for living lead to?

In Disney's *The Lion King,* Scar, the villain, is selfish, ambitious and a liar. These things lead him to murder his brother. Show some short clips from films, discussing the impact of values on bad behaviour in particular.

Bad thoughts? Bad words? Bad actions?

Ask pupils whether there are such things as naughty thoughts. Discuss whether jealousy, hatred, being greedy and so on start in our minds, and sometimes lead to actions as well.

Films again provide a reference point: the thought is often the beginning of the deed.

A guide to naughtiness

Ask pupils in pairs to make lists of 10 things they think are naughty. They should include naughty words, thoughts and deeds.

- What are the effects or consequences of these naughty things?

Talk about what makes an action naughty. Note that 'naughty' actions, or words, often hurt other people or animals. Do people sometimes hurt themselves when they are naughty?

A fun way to do this is to ask them to make a 'Code for Being Naughty' – Ten Commandments if you will.

Ask pupils to share these with the class, and make it amusing – you could get them to do a code for teachers!

Teach the class that Humanists think we can work out what is naughty by thinking about whether our actions will hurt someone else.

Be good, and you'll be happier – usually!

Talk about the ways that we make rules or principles to help us to be good.

- What rules or principles do the children think make most people happy?

You might teach pupils to notice that other people's happiness is as important as their happiness. Humanism is not a selfish way to live because it is about happiness not just for me, but for all humanity!

Ask pupils to suggest one rule for people to follow if they want a happier world, and make a beautifully lettered 'goodness card' out of it. These can be hung on a mobile in the classroom or school entrance hall.

Codes for living and golden rules

Discuss the idea that a person often has a 'code for living' inside their head or heart that helps them to choose good things and say no to bad things.

As a class, make a collage of a large figure of a person, and each child writes a line of a 'code for living' to stick onto their head or heart.

Remind children that we are learning about Humanism, and Humanist people work out their own rules for living by thinking carefully, and trying not to hurt other people.

Francesca's guide to being naughty

1. Sellotape my big Sister to her bed!

2. Delete all My mums programmes off the TV – eSpecially Coronation Street!

3. Squeez all my Sisters Special paints on to the gloor and mix them up!

4. Make evryone Spaghetti but use Worms!

5. Not clean My teeth for 5 days!

RE Today Services

Activity 3   What codes for living do non–religious people use?

During this activity pupils will:

- learn the word 'Humanist' and its meaning. They will learn that Humanism is an alternative to religions.

- begin to understand that not all people are religious, that non-religious people can have codes for living that don't refer to god, and that a person can be 'good without god'.

What is Humanism? Who is a Humanist?

Discuss with the class the religions they know about, and **ask**

- Is everyone part of a religion?

Many pupils are not. Explore the idea that religious people try to be 'good with God', but others think you can be 'good without god'. Introduce the work of the British Humanist Association (BHA) to pupils.

What do Humanists think is good?

Ask pupils to think about these rules or principles:

- Be honest

- Be generous

- Use your mind

- Tell the truth

- Be thoughtful: think first, then act!

- Do to other people what you would like them to do to you.

Teach pupils that these are the kind of 'rules' or ideals Humanists try to live by. It is good to remember that these are not 'rules' given by a higher authority – but many children of this age group are not ready to distinguish 'rules' from 'ideals' or 'principles' yet, so don't get hung up on this point. **Ask** pupils if they can rank the six rules above in two ways:

- More important to less important?

- Hardest to keep, easier to keep?

Are they actually all connected, and equally hard or important?

- What would happen if everyone in the school, or the town, or the world, lived like this?

- What if everyone did the opposite of this?

Activity 4   Following values

Refer back to the film clips used in Activity 2.

- Were any of the characters you looked at from Disney following Humanist values?

- How could you tell?

Ask children if they can see any **similarities** between Humanist values and what they know of religious values.

Choose two religions that children have studied and compare the values.

Record good answers for reference later in the unit.

Respectful disagreement: an aim in RE

As you would with two different religions, good pedagogy doesn't compare one way of life with another in ways that denigrate one alternative.

This needs careful handling in regard to Humanism: visitors to schools from the BHA have learned to talk thoughtfully about their own way of life, including talking about disagreements over religious ideas. But they don't denigrate, abuse or attack religious people: discussion about beliefs and values can be respectful.

Activity 5   Sorting and ranking Humanist children's ideas

Give pairs of pupils page 28 cut into nine cards.

Ask pupils to organise them into the pattern called 'Diamond Nine', by discussing each opinion.

- Which of the comments do they most agree with?

- Least agree with?

Most agree with

Least agree with

Nine opinions

We asked some Humanist and Atheist pupils aged 9–13 what they thought about the values that really matter to them.

- With your partner, take a copy of the nine replies here and cut it up into nine cards.
- Arrange them into a Diamond Nine with cards you most agree with at the top and cards you least agree with at the bottom.

```
      X
    X   X
  X   X   X
    X   X
      X
```

I learned my values from my mum and dad, from the books I read and my grandparents. I think my own thoughts too, when I see and hear my friends – I think about their behaviour. When I grow up I would like to be a judge and help make laws, so things can be fairer for people. Children don't have to feel bad if they say they don't believe in God. It should be allowed to say you don't believe in things.

Nine-year-old girl: Humanist

My parents have mostly taught me about love, forgiveness, justice and other values. I have learnt sometimes you do have to forgive someone for what they have done. I also learnt to be truthful about a lot of things. Plus I have learnt that actually every single one of those things you do with love are the best things you do in life.

Ten-year-old boy: Humanist

I've learnt my values from my parents, my friends, my family and my teachers. I've learnt that everyone has a right to freedom, truth, justice, love and forgiveness, but this doesn't always happen. If we want the world to be a better place then we should try to do these things ourselves.

Eleven-year-old girl: Atheist

I think it is important to find out about everyone's beliefs. It is interesting and shows that you respect their ideas as well as your own. I think it is strange that Hindus believe in reincarnation. I also found out that some Muslims kill an animal for Eid. I was shocked at first but they said it was done painlessly by the butcher and then shared with the poor, for food, which I actually think is a really good way of celebrating!"

Eleven-year-old girl: Atheist

I personally do not believe in God or Jesus, but I would not do something like be disrespectful or mean to people who do believe in them. I wouldn't insult people because of their beliefs because everyone is different and that is not a bad thing and I would not be rude about God or Jesus. I know many people who believe in God and I also know that many more do too – just not me – but it's OK.

Eleven-year-old girl: Atheist

I think the best way to live is not to believe in anything, really, have no boundaries; therefore when mistakes happen, you don't have to pray for forgiveness. But I reckon everyone knows the difference between good and evil, or can interpret it, so that could be one boundary, staying way from all evil!

Thirteen-year-old girl: Atheist

I have learnt a lot about religions and what certain religious people do.

I like all of RE and we have a great teacher. RE is now one of my favourite lessons and I enjoy it a lot.

Eleven-year-old boy: Humanist

I like RE. It helps me find out about other cultures and religions. I have also found out about how other people live, and what they do in their religion. I have also learned to be happy with what I've got, because there are a lot more people in the world less fortunate than me.

Thirteen-year-old girl: Atheist

I have no religious beliefs. I think the best way to live is by relaxing and enjoying life as it comes. You don't live for ever, so make the most of life!

Ten-year-old boy

RE Today Services

Activity 6   What can we learn from playing around with values?

During this activity pupils will:

- use speaking and listening strategies to clarify the values that matter most to each pupil, and explore the fact that different people have different values.

Part A: A values sorting activity

Give pupils a set of cards listing 21 valuable things, including the values of Humanists (see below).

Ask pupils in groups of three or four to sort the cards into three groups of seven.

You could give the pupils three circles to put them in:

(a) things that really matter a lot

(b) things that are quite valuable

(c) things that don't matter to them.

Ask pupils to say why they have selected the ones that they put in the first group

- What makes these things most valuable?

Discuss as a class:

- which five values they think a Humanist would put in the first group, and why
- which five might a Humanist not be too bothered about? Why?

Compile the answers to this on the whiteboard, in a three circles chart, to share ideas around the class.

Ask pupils to complete a writing task that identifies their own five 'matters most to me' valuable things.

- For each of the five, can they say why it's significant?

Part B: A values auction

Use the same class groups of three or four, and give each group a pretend budget of £100.

The teacher as auctioneer needs a hammer, and sells off the 21 valuable things to the groups for the highest prices a group will bid.

To prevent chaos:

- only allow one child from each group to bid out loud
- others in the group can whisper advice, keep count of the money, make sure other groups are not going to outbid them and so on
- fine offenders £1!

The auction is a highly exciting setting for learning, and you may find it helpful as auctioneer to have another adult in the room for this lesson. Expect it to be a fun, noisy environment, and let the action flow.

We have put a recording sheet for the groups to use on the RE Today members' website – download it if you're a member (password is inside the back of each term's *REtoday* magazine). It helps pupils understand and make a record of what they are doing.

Afterwards, consider together why so many of these values ideas are worth more than money.

(**w**)

Acknowledgement: RE Today would like to thank Mike Lake of Derby Humanists for his generous help in improving this article.

Twenty-one valuable things?

Food	Friends	Being safe	The Xbox	My computer	Football	Music
Pets	Kind-ness	Life after death	Science	Learning	Money	Family
Being loved	Air and water	Exercise	Being healthy	God	Worship	Honesty

Representing Buddhism: tips for teachers

In general

Buddhism is a global belief system with followers all over the world. Ensure that the diversity of the community is shown: those from the West who have adopted Buddhist practice and those for whom it has been the family belief system for generations, for example many people from Thailand.

Buddhism was founded by Siddhattha Gotama (Siddhartha Gautama) in the sixth century BCE. He became known as the Buddha, the enlightened one. A Buddha is not a god, but someone who has achieved awakening from the suffering of ordinary life and helps others to reach Enlightenment. He is not worshipped or prayed to. He is honoured and followed as an example.

When teaching any religion or belief system it is important to look not only at celebrations, but also at beliefs, teaching and practice and the effect that they have on the life of a believer. The teachings of the Buddha are referred to as the Dhamma (Dharma).

Teaching: The Four Noble Truths

The Buddha set out the Four Noble Truths in his first sermon.

1 **Dukkha (Duhkha)** – dis-ease, unsatisfactoriness, imperfection, suffering [*the illness*]

2 **Samudaya** – craving (*tanha*) and ignorance, the origins of dukkha [*the cause of the illness*]

3 **Nirodha** – the cessation of dukkha, Nibbana (Nirvana) [*the cure*]

4 **Magga (Marga)** – the path leading to the cessation of dukkha, the Middle Way; the Noble Eightfold Path [*the remedy*].

The Four Noble Truths are fundamental to all Buddhist teachings; it is from these that all else follows. They are to be understood as a whole. The first three analyse the human condition, likening it to an illness, and the fourth affirms the remedy.

See: http://bit.ly/1IHJop

Devotion

Buddhists regularly practise meditation as well other devotions. In class it is not appropriate to 'do meditation' with pupils in the same way we would not pray in the RE classroom.

Teaching: The Noble Eightfold Path

Following the Noble Eightfold Path provides a way of life that can lead to Enlightenment and an end to suffering.

Wisdom

1 **Right Understanding** – seeing that the Buddha's teachings are right

2 **Right Intention** – giving up worldly desires (non-attachment)

Ethical conduct

3 **Right Speech** – speaking in a positive way, avoiding lies and gossip

4 **Right Action** – not harming any living thing

5 **Right Livelihood** – avoiding taking jobs which harm living creatures

Mental discipline

6 **Right Effort** – making a conscious effort to encourage positive thoughts

7 **Right Mindfulness** – becoming more aware of the self (body, feelings, and mind) and the surroundings

8 **Right Concentration** – practising meditation to enable the mind to become calm, to develop loving kindness and to gain insights into the truths of life.

See: http://bit.ly/J6P9le

Teaching: The Five Precepts

The precepts are personal ethical guidance for Buddhists to follow which will help them on the Noble Eightfold Path. Ordained Buddhists have additional precepts to consider, the number depending on the branch of Buddhism

1 **Not harming** any living beings – trying to show more loving kindness and concern for all life.

2 **Not stealing** – trying to be more generous in thoughts, words and deeds.

3 **Not practising** sexual misconduct – practising stillness, simplicity and contentment.

4 **Not speaking cruelly** or telling lies – trying to speak the truth and say kind and helpful things.

5 **Not taking drink or drugs** that stop you thinking clearly – trying to be aware of all your thoughts, words and deeds.

See: http://bit.ly/1ObjRQ

Spelling of key terms

Key Buddhist terms are given first in Pali with the Sanskrit form following in brackets e.g. Kamma (Karma) and Dukkha (Duhkha). Pali is the language of the texts of the Theravada school, whilst Sanskrit is used in the Mahayana school.

RE Today
Services

Representing Humanism: tips for teachers

In general

RE is for pupils who do not identify with a faith tradition as much as for those with a faith background. In RE we therefore need to consider appropriate alternative belief systems to religion that exist in modern Britain. It is not only religions that regard ethics as central to life: there are many philosophies that encourage their followers to live life mindful of others' needs. These different philosophies are sometimes grouped under the title of non-religious ethical life stances.

Atheist – a person who feels no personal need to propose the existence of gods in order to answer the big questions of life – Where did everything come from? What happens after death? What is the meaning of life? Atheists do their best to lead happy and morally responsible lives free from all the trappings of religious belief.

Agnostic – someone who doesn't know or has an open mind about religious beliefs and in particular about the existence of God.

Humanist – a definition is offered on the British Humanist Association (BHA) website: www.humanism.org.uk

A Humanist is someone who:

- trusts to the scientific method when it comes to understanding how the universe works and rejects the idea of the supernatural (and is therefore an atheist or agnostic)

- makes ethical decisions based on reason, empathy, and a concern for human beings and other sentient animals

- believes that, in the absence of an afterlife and any discernible purpose to the universe, human beings can act to give their own lives meaning by seeking happiness in this life and helping others to do the same.

The golden rule

Humanists believe it is a reasoned sense of goodness that should support decision-making of the right path to follow for individuals and other people. When considering ethics and ethical decisions, Humanists believe we should look at individual cases, considering carefully the individual situation and the effect of possible choices on the wellbeing of people, animals, the environment and the wider community. When making ethical decisions Humanists try to follow the Golden Rule – treat other people as you would like them to treat you.

See: http://bit.ly/k0vHYw

Human nature

Humanists believe that human nature is remarkable but not created by god or any other divine being. People must rely on humanity not god to support them in life; thus human reason, goodwill and science are the key to dealing with life's issues and dilemmas. Humanists value justice, freedom and happiness as positive values and aims in life. Humanists do not refer to religious texts or authorities when making moral decisions, but to their own reason.

Living life responsibly

Humanists believe we should enjoy the positive things in life if it is possible to do that without harming the environment or other people. Humanists believe it is important to make responsible choices. Humanists believe in active citizenship and will often be found campaigning against something they have decided is unjust.

See: www.humanism.org.uk

Celebrating

Secular ceremonies for weddings, baby welcoming and funerals are popular for Humanists and others who want to celebrate or mark these significant life events without using religious texts, buildings or leaders. There are generally local celebrants and the British Humanist Association provides texts to support these ceremonies.

See: www.humanism.org.uk/ ceremonies

Studying Humanism

A more formal study of Humanism might include reference to beliefs and values, finding out about Humanist ceremonies and ethical activities and – for older pupils – learning about contemporary Humanist figures.

See: www.humanismforschools org.uk

Representing Sikhism: tips for teachers

In general

In Britain today there are over 350,000 Sikhs, making it the largest Sikh community outside the Punjab. The first Sikh gurdwara was opened in 1911 in Shepherd's Bush. There are substantial Sikh populations in Greater London (especially Southall), Birmingham, Coventry, Leicester, Wolverhampton, Bradford, Cardiff and Glasgow. Worldwide there are over 23 million Sikhs, living mostly in the Punjab but also spread all over the world.

Guru Nanak, the first of the ten Sikh Gurus, lived in the Punjab region of India over 500 years ago. When he was about 30, he received the call to preach the word of God, and travelled extensively to fulfil this mission. Sikhism is seen as an original, revealed religion.

When teaching any religion or belief system it is important to look not only at celebrations, but also at beliefs, teaching and practice and the effect that they have on the life of a believer. The Ten Gurus each contributed something to the developing faith and way of life that is the Sikh **dharma**. **Guru Gobind Singh** declared that he was the last human Guru and that the **Guru Granth Sahib (Sikh scriptures)** was to be their living Guru.

Sikh belief: God

The oneness of God

- The belief that there is one God is central to Sikhism. God is Eternal, Truth, and Creator. God is both transcendent and immanent.

- These beliefs are reflected in the Mool Mantar, the opening passage of the Guru Granth Sahib. The Mool Mantar is recited regularly by Sikhs in their private and public worship.

Names for God

- **Sat Nam** – the Eternal Reality
- **Akal Purakh** – the Eternal One
- **Raheguru** – Wonderful Lord

Nam Simran

- The practice of remembering and meditating on the name of God.

See: http://sikhs.org

See: www.bbc.co.uk/religion/religions/sikhism

Sikh belief: Ethics

Equality

Sikhs believe in the oneness of humanity. All people are equal, regardless of gender, age, wealth, social class, religion or belief.

Sikhs show their belief in equality in many ways: for example, anyone can eat in the langar, the free kitchen provided after every service in the gurdwara.

Sewa (Seva)

For Sikhs life is about service (sewa) to God, to the Khalsa and to humanity in general.

There are three types of service:

- **Physical (Tan)**: service to the community, for example, preparing and serving food in the langar; cleaning the shoes of the worshippers

- **Mental (Man)**: service to the Guru: for example, teaching children about Sikhism; showing adults round the gurdwara

- **Material (Dhan)**: giving money or goods to charitable causes; giving your time to help those in need.

Honest work (Kirat Karna)

Sikhs should take part in honest work. This is work that is needed for the good of both the family and the wider community. Work should not exploit others. This links with the ideas of equality, and of generosity in the use of possessions and time.

Commitment: The Five Ks

In 1699 Guru Gobind Singh, the tenth Guru, instituted the Khalsa, a group of committed Sikhs. To show their commitment they were to wear a number of symbols: the five Ks.

1. **Kesh** – uncut hair. A man, and some women, will cover their uncut hair with a turban.

2. **Kangha** – a small comb which keeps the hair in place.

3. **Kara** – a steel bracelet which is worn on the right wrist. It is a symbol of the oneness of God.

4. **Kachera** – shorts which are worn under clothes to symbolise action. In the Punjab they would have allowed for freedom of movement and modesty.

5. **Kirpan** – a sword which a Sikh should always carry to symbolise the readiness to defend the faith or use against oppression.

Sikhs who join the Khalsa take part in an initiation ceremony called the Amrit ceremony. Joining the Khalsa means someone making promises that require a high level of commitment to the faith and in their own personal life. Not all Sikhs will join the Khalsa during their lifetime.

See: www.bbc.co.uk learningzone/clips

- Origin of the Khalsa – clip 672
- The Meaning of the Five Ks – clip 4805
- Explanation of Khanda and Khalsa – clip 4806

RE Today Services